THE P.

CW00539250

by Agatha Christie

|| SAMUEL FRENCH ||

www.concordtheatricals.co.uk
www.concordtheatricals.com
www.agathachristielimited.com

FOR PRODUCTION ENQUIRIES

UNITED KINGDOM AND WORLD
EXCLUDING NORTH AMERICA
licensing@concordtheatricals.co.uk

020-7054-7200

NORTH AMERICA
info@concordtheatricals.com
1-866-979-0447

Each title is subject to availability from Concord Theatricals,
depending upon country of performance.

USE OF COPYRIGHTED MUSIC

A licence issued by Concord Theatricals to perform this play does not include permission to use the incidental music specified in this publication. In the United Kingdom: Where the place of performance is already licensed by the PERFORMING RIGHT SOCIETY (PRS) a return of the music used must be made to them. If the place of performance is not so licensed then application should be made to PRS for Music (www.prsformusic.com). A separate and additional licence from PHONOGRAPHIC PERFORMANCE LTD (www. ppluk.com) may be needed whenever commercial recordings are used. Outside the United Kingdom: Please contact the appropriate music licensing authority in your territory for the rights to any incidental music.

USE OF COPYRIGHTED THIRD-PARTY MATERIALS

Licensees are solely responsible for obtaining formal written permission from copyright owners to use copyrighted third-party materials (e.g., artworks, logos) in the performance of this play and are strongly cautioned to do so. If no such permission is obtained by the licensee, then the licensee must use only original materials that the licensee owns and controls. Licensees are solely responsible and liable for clearances of all third-party copyrighted materials, and shall indemnify the copyright owners of the play(s) and their licensing agent, Concord Theatricals Ltd., against any costs, expenses, losses and liabilities arising from the use of such copyrighted third-party materials by licensees.

IMPORTANT BILLING AND CREDIT REQUIREMENTS

If you have obtained performance rights to this title, please refer to your licensing agreement for important billing and credit requirements.

CHARACTERS

LANSEN
NURSE
DR. GINSBERG
INSPECTOR CRAY
BRYAN WINGFIELD
EMMELINE ROSS
WILLIAM ROSS
BRENDA JACKSON
THE PATIENT

THE PATIENT was first presented by Peter Saunders at the Duchess Theatre, London on December 29, 1962. The director was Hubert Gregg, with sets by Peter Rice. The cast was as follows:

LANSEN.. Raymond Bowers

NURSE... Mercy Haystead

DR. GINSBERG.. Robert Raglan

INSPECTOR CRAY... David Langhn

BRYAN WINGFIELD .... Michael Beint

EMMELINE ROSS .... Vera Cook

WILLIAM ROSS... Robin May

BRENDA JACKSON.. Betty McDowall

THE PATIENT.. Rosemary Martin

(A private room in a nursing home. The room is plain and hygienic looking. There is a set of double doors leading to other parts of the nursing home and across the back a large window covered by Venetian blinds which are at present down but not closed. There is also a small alcove which currently has a curtain drawn across it. There is a piece of electrical apparatus with dials and a red light, a hospital trolley with a steriliser on top and a wall telephone with a bell next to it. There is also a small table with an elbow chair next to it and four small chairs in a rough semicircle. These chairs have the appearance of having been brought into the room for a purpose and not really belonging to it. LANSEN, a tall, gangling young man with spectacles, wearing a long white hospital overall, is fiddling with the electrical apparatus. The NURSE, a tall, good-looking woman, competent and correct, is at the trolley. She lifts the lid of the steriliser, removes a needle with some forceps then places it on a tray. Crossing to the alcove she draws back the curtain, takes out a towel and crosses back to the trolley. A buzzer sounds. DR. GINSBERG enters through the double doors. He is a dark, clever looking man in his mid-forties. He makes for the telephone.)

GINSBERG. All right, Nurse, I'll answer it.

(He picks up the telephone.)

Yes? ...Oh, Inspector Cray, good. Ask him to come up to Room Fourteen, will you?

(He puts down the telephone and crosses to **LANSEN** *and the electrical apparatus.)*

GINSBERG. How are you doing, Lansen? Got it fixed up?

LANSEN. Yes, everything's in order. I'll plug in here, Dr. Ginsberg.

GINSBERG. You're quite sure about this, now? We can't afford to have a slip-up.

LANSEN. Quite sure, Doctor. It'll work a treat.

GINSBERG. Good.

(He turns and looks at the chairs.)

Oh, a little less formal I think, Nurse. Let's move these chairs a bit.

(He moves one to the corner.)

Er – that one over there against the wall.

NURSE. Yes, Doctor.

*(**GINSBERG** exits. The **NURSE** lifts a chair, almost hitting the electrical apparatus.)*

LANSEN. Careful!

*(He takes the chair from her and places it against the wall. The **NURSE** looks over the apparatus with curiosity.)*

NURSE. What is this thing?

LANSEN. *(Grinning.)* New electrical gadget.

NURSE. *(Bored.)* Oh, one of those.

LANSEN. Trouble with you people is you've no respect for science.

*(**INSPECTOR CRAY** enters. He is a middle-aged man of delusively mild appearance. **GINSBERG** follows.)*

INSPECTOR. Good afternoon.

GINSBERG. Everything's ready.

*(The **INSPECTOR** approaches **LANSEN** at the apparatus.)*

INSPECTOR. Is this the contraption?

LANSEN. Good afternoon, Inspector.

GINSBERG. Yes. It's been well tested, Inspector.

LANSEN. It works perfectly. The least touch will make a connection. I guarantee there will be no hitch.

GINSBERG. All right, Lansen. We'll call you when we need you.

(**LANSEN** *exits*. **GINSBERG** *turns to the* **NURSE**.)

Has Nurse Cartwright got the patient ready?

NURSE. Yes, Doctor. Quite ready.

GINSBERG. Nurse Bond here is going to stay and assist me during the experiment.

INSPECTOR. Oh, good. That's very kind of you.

NURSE. Not at all, Inspector. I'll do anything I can to help. I'd never have gone off duty if I'd thought that Mrs. Wingfield was unduly depressed.

GINSBERG. Nobody's blaming you, Nurse.

(*He turns to the* **INSPECTOR**.)

You say the others have arrived?

INSPECTOR. Yes, they're downstairs.

GINSBERG. All four of them?

INSPECTOR. All four of them. Bryan Wingfield, Emmeline Ross, William Ross and Brenda Jackson. They can't leave, I've posted my men.

GINSBERG. (*Formally.*) You must understand Inspector, that the wellbeing of my patient comes before anything else. At the first sign of collapse or undue excitement, any indication that the experiment is having an adverse effect, I shall stop the proceedings.

(*He turns to the* **NURSE**.)

You understand that, Nurse?

NURSE. Yes, Doctor.

INSPECTOR. Quite so, quite so, I shouldn't expect anything else. (*Uneasily.*) You don't think it's too risky?

GINSBERG. *(Coldly.)* If I thought it was too risky I should not permit the experiment. Mrs. Wingfield's condition is mainly psychological, the result of severe shock. Her temperature, heart and pulse are now normal. Nurse, you are already acquainted with the family. Go down to the waiting room and bring them up here. If they ask you any questions please be strictly non-committal in your answers.

NURSE. Yes, Doctor.

 (The NURSE exits.)

INSPECTOR. Well, here we go.

GINSBERG. Yes.

INSPECTOR. Let's hope we have luck. Have any of them been allowed to see her?

GINSBERG. Her husband, naturally. And also her brother and sister for a few minutes. The nurse assigned to look after her here, Nurse Cartwright, was present all the time.

 (He pauses.)

Miss Jackson has not visited Mrs. Wingfield, nor asked to do so.

INSPECTOR. Quite so. You'll give them a little preliminary talk, will you? Put them in the picture.

GINSBERG. Certainly, if you wish. I see that Mrs. Wingfield fell from the second storey balcony.

INSPECTOR. Yes. Yes, she did.

GINSBERG. Remarkable really, that she wasn't killed. Head contusions, dislocated shoulder and fracture of the left leg.

 (The NURSE enters. She holds the door open and BRYAN WINGFIELD, WILLIAM ROSS and EMMELINE ROSS enter. WINGFIELD is a short, stocky man of about thirty-five, attractive, with a quiet manner and a poker face. WILLIAM ROSS is a man of the same age, also short, but dark-haired, rather mercurial in

temperament. **EMMELINE**, *his sister, is a tall, grim-faced woman of forty. They are all in a state of emotional disturbance. The* **NURSE** *exits.* **GINSBERG** *shakes hands with them in turn.)*

Good afternoon, Miss Ross, will you sit down?

(She does so. He turns to **MR. ROSS** *and finally* **WINGFIELD**.*)*

Mr. Ross! Good afternoon. Mr. Wingfield.

WINGFIELD. You sent for us – it's not – my wife? There's not bad news?

GINSBERG. No, Mr. Wingfield. No bad news.

WINGFIELD. Thank God. When you sent for us I thought there might be a change for the worse.

GINSBERG. There is no change of any kind, neither for the worse nor, alas, for the better.

EMMELINE. Is my sister still unconscious?

GINSBERG. She is still completely paralysed. She cannot move or speak.

EMMELINE. It's terrible. Simply terrible!

INSPECTOR. Was Miss Jackson with you?

WINGFIELD. She was following us.

*(**BRENDA JACKSON** enters. She is a tall, extremely pretty young woman of twenty-five.)*

Dr. Ginsberg, my secretary, Miss Jackson.

GINSBERG. Good afternoon.

*(**WINGFIELD** indicates a chair and* **BRENDA** *crosses to it. She eyes the electrical apparatus.)*

ROSS. Poor Jenny, what an awful thing to happen to anyone. Sometimes I feel it would have been better if she'd been killed outright by the fall.

WINGFIELD. No. Anything but that.

ROSS. I know what you feel, Bryan. But this – I mean, it's a living death isn't it, Doctor?

GINSBERG. There's still some hope for your sister, Mr. Ross.

BRENDA. But she won't stay like this? I mean – she'll get better won't she?

GINSBERG. In cases of this kind it is very difficult to forecast the progress of a patient. Her injuries will heal, yes. The bones will knit, the dislocation has already been reduced, the wounds in the head are nearly healed.

WINGFIELD. Then why shouldn't she get well? Why shouldn't she be herself again in every way?

GINSBERG. You are touching there on a field in which we are still ignorant. Mrs. Wingfield's state of paralysis is due to shock.

EMMELINE. The result of her accident?

GINSBERG. Her accident was the ostensible cause.

ROSS. Just what do you mean by ostensible?

GINSBERG. Mrs. Wingfield must have suffered unusual fears before she fell from the balcony. It is not so much her *physical* injuries but something in her *mind* that has produced this state of complete paralysis.

(**BRENDA** *sits.*)

WINGFIELD. You're not trying to say – you're not thinking what I'm sure the Inspector has been more or less suggesting, that my wife tried to commit suicide? That I don't believe for a moment.

INSPECTOR. I haven't said I thought it was suicide, Mr. Wingfield.

WINGFIELD. You must think something of the kind or you and your people wouldn't keep hanging round like vultures.

INSPECTOR. We have to be quite clear as to the cause of this – accident.

ROSS. (*Impatiently.*) My God, isn't it simple enough? She's been ill for months. She'd been feeling weak, up for the first time, or practically the first time. Goes over to the window, out on to the balcony, leans over, is suddenly taken giddy and falls to the ground. That balcony's very low.

EMMELINE. Don't get so excited William, don't shout.

ROSS. It's all very well, Bunny, but it makes me mad all this business.

(He turns to **GINSBERG**.*)*

Do you think it's pleasant for us having the police mixing themselves up in our family affairs?

WINGFIELD. Now Bill, if anyone should complain it's myself and I don't.

BRENDA. What have we been asked to come here for?

INSPECTOR. One moment, Miss Jackson.

(He turns to **EMMELINE**.*)*

Miss Ross, I wish you could tell me a little more about your sister. Was she at all subject to fits of melancholy – depression?

EMMELINE. She was always highly strung, nervous.

ROSS. Oh, I wouldn't say that at all.

EMMELINE. Men don't realise these things. I know what I'm talking about. I think it is quite possible, Inspector, that her illness had left her particularly low and depressed and that with other things she had to worry and distress her...

*(***BRENDA*** rises and makes to exit. Everyone turns. The* **INSPECTOR** *stops her.)*

INSPECTOR. Where are you going, Miss Jackson?

BRENDA. I'm leaving. I'm not one of the family, I'm only Mr. Wingfield's secretary. I don't see the point of all this. I was asked to come with the others, but if all you're going to do is to go over and over again about the accident – whether it was accident or attempted suicide – well, I don't see why I should stay.

INSPECTOR. But it's not going to be the same thing over and over again, Miss Jackson. We are about to make an experiment.

BRENDA. *(Arrested.)* An experiment? What kind of experiment?

INSPECTOR. Dr. Ginsberg will explain. Sit down, Miss Jackson.

 (**BRENDA** *moves back to her chair and sits.*)

Dr. Ginsberg!

GINSBERG. I had better perhaps recapitulate what I know or have been told. Mrs. Wingfield has been suffering in the last two months from an illness somewhat mysterious in nature which was puzzling the doctor in attendance on her, Dr. Horsefield. This I have on the authority of Dr. Horsefield himself. She was however, showing decided signs of improvement and was convalescent, though there was still a nurse in the house. On the day in question, exactly ten days ago, Mrs. Wingfield got up from bed after lunch and was settled by Nurse Bond in an easy chair near the open window, it being a fine, mild afternoon. She had books beside her and a small radio. After seeing her patient had all she needed, Nurse went out for her afternoon walk as usual. What happened during the course of the afternoon is a matter of conjecture. But at half past three a cry was heard. Miss Ross, who was sitting in the room below, saw a falling body cross the window. It was the body of Mrs. Wingfield, who had fallen from the balcony of her room. There was no one with her at the time when she fell but there were four people in the house, the four people who are assembled here now.

INSPECTOR. Perhaps, Mr. Wingfield, you would like to tell us in your own words just what happened then?

WINGFIELD. I should have thought I'd told it often enough already. I was correcting proofs in my study. I heard a scream, a noise from outside. I rushed to the side door, went out on the terrace and found – and found poor Jenny.

 (*He turns away.*)

Emmeline joined me a moment later and then William and Miss Jackson. We telephoned for the doctor and I – I –

(His voice breaks.)

INSPECTOR. Yes, yes, Mr. Wingfield, there's no need to go into any more.

*(He turns to **BRENDA**.)*

Miss Jackson, will you tell us again your side of the story?

BRENDA. I had been asked to look up a reference in the encyclopaedia for Mr. Wingfield. I was in the library when I heard a commotion and people running. I dropped the book and came out and joined them on the terrace.

*(The **INSPECTOR** turns to **ROSS**.)*

INSPECTOR. Mr. Ross?

ROSS. What? Oh – I'd been playing golf all the morning, always play golf on a Saturday. I'd come in, eaten a hearty lunch and was feeling whacked. I lay down on my bed upstairs. It was Jenny's scream that woke me up. I thought for a moment I must have been dreaming. Then I heard the row down below and I looked out of my window. There she was on the terrace with the others gathered round. *(Fiercely.)* Oh God, have we got to go over this again and again?

INSPECTOR. I only wanted to stress the point that nobody who was in the house can tell us exactly what happened that afternoon.

(He pauses.)

Nobody, that is, except Mrs. Wingfield herself.

ROSS. It's all perfectly simple, as I've said all along. Poor Jenny thought she was stronger than she was. She went out on the balcony, leant over, and that's that. Perfectly simple accident, might have happened to anybody.

WINGFIELD. Somebody ought to have been with her. I blame myself for leaving her alone.

EMMELINE. But she was supposed to rest in the afternoon Bryan, that was part of the doctor's orders. We were all going to join her at half past four for tea, but she was supposed to rest every afternoon from three o'clock until then.

INSPECTOR. Miss Ross, the accident seems a little difficult to explain. The railings of the balcony did not give way.

ROSS. No, no. She got giddy and overbalanced. I leant over myself to test it afterwards and it could easily happen.

INSPECTOR. Mrs. Wingfield is a very small woman. It wouldn't be so easy for her to overbalance even if she was taken giddy.

EMMELINE. I hate to say it, but I think you're right in what you suspect. I think poor Jenny was worried and troubled in her mind. I think a fit of depression came over her –

WINGFIELD. You keep saying she tried to commit suicide. I don't believe it. I won't believe it.

EMMELINE. *(Significantly.)* She had plenty to make her depressed.

WINGFIELD. What do you mean by that?

EMMELINE. *(Rising.)* I think you know quite well what I mean. I'm not blind, Bryan.

WINGFIELD. Jenny wasn't depressed. She'd nothing to be depressed about. You've got an evil mind Emmeline and you just imagine things.

ROSS. Leave my sister alone.

(BRENDA *rises.*)

BRENDA. It was an accident. Of course it was an accident. Miss Ross is just trying to – trying to –

EMMELINE. Yes, what am I trying to do?

BRENDA. It's women like you that write anonymous letters – poison pen letters. Just because no man has ever looked at you.

EMMELINE. How dare you!

ROSS. Oh my God! Women! Cut it out, both of you.

WINGFIELD. I think we're all rather overexcited, you know. We're talking about things that are quite beside the point. What we really want to get at is what was Jenny's state of mind on the day she fell? Well, I'm her husband, I know her pretty well and I don't think for a moment she meant to commit suicide.

EMMELINE. Because you don't want to think so – you don't want to feel responsible!

WINGFIELD. Responsible? What do you mean by responsible?

EMMELINE. Driving her to do what she did!

(Everyone speaks simultaneously.)

ROSS. What do you mean by that?

WINGFIELD. How dare you!

BRENDA. It's not true!

*(**GINSBERG** silences them.)*

GINSBERG. Please – please! When I asked you to come here, it was not my object to provoke recriminations.

ROSS. *(Angrily.)* Wasn't it? I'm not so sure.

*(He looks suspiciously at the **INSPECTOR**.)*

GINSBERG. No, what I had in mind was to conduct an experiment.

BRENDA. We've already been told that, but you still haven't told us what kind of experiment.

GINSBERG. As Inspector Cray said just now, only one person knows what happened that afternoon – Mrs. Wingfield herself.

WINGFIELD. *(Sighing.)* And she can't tell us. It's too bad.

EMMELINE. She will when she's better.

GINSBERG. I don't think you quite appreciate the medical position, Miss Ross.

*(He crosses to the electrical apparatus. **BRENDA** sits.)*

It may be months, it may even be years before Mrs. Wingfield comes out of this state.

WINGFIELD. Surely not.

GINSBERG. Yes, Mr. Wingfield. I won't go into a lot of medical details, but there are people who have gone blind as a result of shock and have not recovered their sight for fifteen or twenty years. There have been those paralysed and unable to walk for the same periods of time. Sometimes another shock precipitates recovery. But there's no fixed rule.

> (*He turns to the* INSPECTOR.)

Ring the bell, please.

> (*The* INSPECTOR *crosses and rings the bell.*)

WINGFIELD. I don't quite understand what you are driving at Doctor.

> (*He looks from* GINSBERG *to the* INSPECTOR.)

INSPECTOR. You're about to find out, Mr. Wingfield.

> (GINSBERG *crosses to the window and closes the Venetian blinds.*)

GINSBERG. Inspector, do you mind?

> (*The* INSPECTOR *switches on the lights.* LANSEN *opens the doors and pulls on a trolley carrying the* PATIENT. *The* NURSE *follows. The* PATIENT's *head is heavily bandaged, nothing of the features show but the eyes and nose. Her eyes are open but she is quite motionless.*)

WINGFIELD. Jenny, darling!

> (WINGFIELD *moves to her side.* LANSEN *collects the electrical apparatus and moves it nearer.*)

BRENDA. What's going on? What are you trying to do?

GINSBERG. Mrs. Wingfield, as I have told you, is completely paralysed. She cannot move or speak. But we are all agreed that she knows what happened to her on that day.

BRENDA. She's unconscious. She may be unconscious – oh – for years, you said.

GINSBERG. I did not say unconscious. Mrs. Wingfield cannot move and cannot speak but she *can* see and hear. I think it highly probable that her mind is as keen as ever it was. She knows what happened. She would like to communicate it to us but unfortunately she can't do so.

WINGFIELD. You think she can hear us? You think she does know what we are saying to her, what we're feeling?

GINSBERG. I think she knows.

WINGFIELD. Jenny! Jenny, darling! Can you hear me? It's been terrible for you, I know, but everything's going to be all right.

GINSBERG. Lansen?

> (**LANSEN** *is making final adjustments to the electrical apparatus.*)

LANSEN. I'm ready, sir, when you are.

GINSBERG. I said Mrs. Wingfield could not communicate with us but it is possible that a way has been found. Dr. Zalzbergen, who has been attending her and who is a specialist on this form of paralysis, became aware of a very slight power of movement in the fingers of the right hand. It is very slight, hardly noticeable. She could not raise her arm or lift anything but she can very slightly move the two fingers and thumb of her right hand. Mr. Lansen here has fixed up a certain apparatus of an electrical nature.

> (**ROSS** *moves closer to the trolley.*)

You see, there is a small rubber bulb. When that bulb is pressed a red light appears on the top of the apparatus. The slightest pressure will operate it. If you please, Lansen!

> (**LANSEN** *presses the bulb twice. The red light flashes twice.*)

GINSBERG. Nurse, uncover the patient's right arm. Lansen, between the thumb and two fingers. Gently.

(The NURSE lays the PATIENT's arm on the coverlet. LANSEN places the bulb in her hand and crosses to the electrical apparatus.)

Now I'm going to ask Mrs. Wingfield some questions.

ROSS. Ask her questions? What do you mean? Questions about what?

GINSBERG. Questions about what happened on that Saturday afternoon.

(ROSS turns to the INSPECTOR.)

ROSS. This is your doing!

GINSBERG. The experiment was suggested by Mr. Lansen and myself.

WINGFIELD. But you can't possibly put any reliance on what might be purely muscular spasms.

GINSBERG. I think we can soon find out whether Mrs. Wingfield can answer questions or not.

WINGFIELD. I won't have it! It's dangerous for her. It'll set her recovery back. I won't allow this! I won't agree to it.

BRENDA. *(Warningly.)* Bryan!

(She turns to face WINGFIELD then senses the INSPECTOR watching her and sits.)

GINSBERG. Mrs. Wingfield's health will be fully safeguarded, I assure you. Nurse!

(The NURSE places her fingers on the PATIENT's wrist, taking the pulse.)

At the least sign of collapse, you know what to do.

NURSE. Yes, Doctor.

(BRENDA speaks almost under her breath.)

BRENDA. I don't like this – I don't like it.

EMMELINE. I'm sure you don't like it.

BRENDA. Do you?

EMMELINE. I think it might be interesting.

(They speak simultaneously.)

ROSS. I don't believe for a –

WINGFIELD. Inspector, I hope –

INSPECTOR. Quiet, please! We must have absolute quiet. The doctor is about to begin.

(There is a pause.)

GINSBERG. Mrs. Wingfield, you have had a very narrow escape from death and are now on the way to recovery. Your physical injuries are healing. We know that you are paralysed and that you cannot speak or move. What I want is this – if you understand what I am saying to you, try and move your fingers so that you press the bulb. Will you do so?

*(There is a pause. The red light comes on. There is a collective gasp. The **INSPECTOR** now watches them very closely.)*

You have heard and understood what we have been saying, Mrs. Wingfield?

(One red light.)

Thank you. Now what I propose is this: when the answer to a question is "yes" you press the bulb once, if the answer is "no" you will press it twice. Do you understand?

(One red light.)

Now, Mrs. Wingfield, what is the signal for "no"?

(Two red lights in succession.)

I think then, it must be clear to all of you that Mrs. Wingfield can understand what I'm saying and can reply to my questions. I'm going back to the afternoon of Saturday the fourteenth. Have you a clear recollection of what happened that afternoon?

(One red light.)

GINSBERG. As far as possible, I will ask you questions that will save you too much fatigue. I am assuming therefore, that you had lunch, got up and that Nurse here settled you in a chair by the window. You were alone in your room with the window open and were supposed to rest until four-thirty. Am I correct?

(One red light.)

Did you in fact, sleep a little?

(One red light.)

And then you woke up?

(One red light.)

Went out on to the balcony?

(One red light.)

You leant over?

(One red light.)

You lost your balance and fell?

*(There is a pause. **LANSEN** bends over to adjust the electrical apparatus.)*

Just a minute, Lansen! You fell?

(One red light.)

But you did not lose your balance.

(Two red lights. A gasp from everyone.)

You were giddy – felt faint?

(Two red lights.)

WINGFIELD. Inspector, I –

INSPECTOR. Sssh!

GINSBERG. Mrs. Wingfield, we have come to the point where you have to tell us what happened. I am going to go over the letters of the alphabet. When I come to the letter of the word you want, will you press the bulb. I'll begin. A, B, C, D, E, F, G, H, I, J, K, L, M, N, O, P.

(One red light.)

You have given me the letter "P." I'm going to hazard a guess – I want you to tell me if I am right. Is the word in your mind "pushed"?

(One red light. There is a general sensation.
BRENDA *shrinks, her face in her hands.* **ROSS**
swears. **EMMELINE** *is still.)*

BRENDA. No, it can't be true!

ROSS. What the hell!

WINGFIELD. This is iniquitous!

GINSBERG. Quiet, please. I cannot have the patient agitated.
Mrs. Wingfield, you obviously have more to tell us. I'm
going to spell again. A, B, C, D, E, F, G, H, I, J, K, L, M.

(One red light.)

M? The letter "M" is probably followed by a vowel.
Which vowel, Mrs. Wingfield? A, E, I, O, U.

(One red light. The **INSPECTOR** *moves to the
electrical apparatus.)*

M-U?

(One red light.)

Is the next letter "R"?

(One red light. The **INSPECTOR** *and* **GINSBERG**
exchange a look.)

M-U-R. Mrs. Wingfield, are you trying to tell us that
what happened that afternoon was not an accident?
Are you trying to tell us that it was attempted murder?

*(One red light. There is an immediate reaction.
Everyone speaks simultaneously.)*

WINGFIELD. It's incredible! Absolutely incredible. It's
impossible, I tell you, impossible!

BRENDA. This is nonsense. Poor Jenny doesn't know what
she's doing.

EMMELINE. It's not true. She doesn't know what she's saying.

ROSS. Murder! Murder! It can't be murder! D'you mean
someone got in?

*(***GINSBERG** *silences them.)*

GINSBERG. Please. Quiet, please!

EMMELINE. She doesn't know what she's saying.

INSPECTOR. I think she does.

GINSBERG. Mrs. Wingfield, did some unknown person come in from outside and attack you?

> *(Two red lights sharply.)*

Was it someone in the house who pushed you?

> *(There is a pause, then one red light.)*

WINGFIELD. My God!

> *(The red light flashes several times.)*

NURSE. Doctor, her pulse is quickening.

> *(The **INSPECTOR** crosses to **GINSBERG**.)*

INSPECTOR. *(Confidentially.)* Not much further. We must have the name.

GINSBERG. Mrs. Wingfield, do you know who pushed you?

> *(One red light.)*

I'm going to spell out the name. Do you understand?

> *(One red light.)*

Good. A, B.

> *(One red light.)*

B. Is that right?

> *(Several red lights.)*

NURSE. Doctor! She's collapsed.

GINSBERG. It's no good. I daren't go on. Nurse!

> *(The **NURSE** goes to the trolley and collects a hypodermic. She hands the syringe to **GINSBERG**.)*

Thank you.

> *(He breaks the ampule head, fills the syringe and injects it in the **PATIENT**'s arm.)*

Lansen.

*(**LANSEN** switches off the electrical apparatus and removes the bulb from the **PATIENT**'s hand. He wheels the electrical apparatus into the curtained recess then exits.)*

Nurse, would you unplug the steriliser?

NURSE. Yes, Doctor.

*(The **NURSE** returns the syringe to the trolley and unplugs the steriliser.)*

WINGFIELD. Is she all right?

GINSBERG. The strain and excitement have been too much for her. She'll be all right. She must rest for a while. We should be able to resume in about half an hour.

WINGFIELD. I forbid you to go on with it. It's dangerous.

GINSBERG. I think you must allow me to be the best judge of that. We'll move Mrs. Wingfield up nearer the window. She'll be all right there.

*(The **NURSE** helps **GINSBERG** and they move the **PATIENT** over to the window.)*

EMMELINE. There's not much doubt is there, who she meant? "B."

*(She turns to **WINGFIELD**.)*

Not much doubt about that is there, Bryan?

WINGFIELD. You always hated me, Emmeline. You always had it in for me. I tell you here and now, I didn't try to kill my wife.

EMMELINE. Do you deny that you were having an affair with that woman there?

*(She points to **BRENDA**.)*

BRENDA. It's not true.

EMMELINE. Don't tell me that. You were head over ears in love with him.

BRENDA. All right, then. I was in love with him. But that was all over ages ago. He didn't really care for me. It's all over, I tell you. All over!

EMMELINE. In that case it seems odd you stayed on as his secretary.

BRENDA. I didn't want to go. I – oh, all right, then! *(Passionately.)* I still wanted to be near him.

EMMELINE. And perhaps you thought that if Jenny were out of the way, you'd console him very nicely and be Mrs. Wingfield Number Two.

WINGFIELD. Emmeline, for heaven's sake!

EMMELINE. Perhaps it's "B" for Brenda.

BRENDA. You horrible woman! I hate you. It's not true.

ROSS. Bryan and Brenda. It seems to narrow it down to one of you two all right.

WINGFIELD. I wouldn't say that. It could be "B" for brother, couldn't it? Or Bill?

ROSS. She always called me William.

WINGFIELD. After all, who stands to gain by poor Jenny's death? Not me. It's you. You and Emmeline. It's you two who get her money.

GINSBERG. Please – please! I can't have all this argument. Nurse, will you take them down to the waiting room.

NURSE. Yes, Doctor.

ROSS. We can't stay cooped up in a little room with all of us slanging each other.

INSPECTOR. You can go where you please on the hospital premises, but none of you is actually to leave the place. *(Sharply.)* Is that understood?

BRYAN. All right.

ROSS. Yes.

EMMELINE. I have no wish to leave. My conscience is clear.

        (**BRENDA** *approaches* **EMMELINE.**)

BRENDA. I think you did it.

EMMELINE. *(Sharply.)* What do you mean?

BRENDA. You hate her, you've always hated her. And you get the money, you and your brother.

EMMELINE. My name does not begin with a "B," I'm thankful to say.

BRENDA. *(Excitedly.)* No but it needn't.

(She turns to the **INSPECTOR**.*)*

Supposing that, after all, Mrs. Wingfield didn't see who it was who pushed her off the balcony.

EMMELINE. She has told us that she did.

BRENDA. But supposing that she didn't. Don't you see what a temptation it might be to her? She was jealous of me and Bryan, oh yes, she knew about us and she was jealous. And when that machine there gave her a chance to get back at us, at me – don't you see how tempting it was to say "Brenda pushed me." It could have been like that, it could!

INSPECTOR. A little far-fetched.

BRENDA. No, it isn't! Not to a jealous woman. You don't know what women are like when they're jealous. And she'd been cooped up there in her room, thinking, suspecting, wondering if Bryan and I were still carrying on together. It isn't far-fetched, I tell you. It could easily be true.

(She looks at **WINGFIELD**.*)*

WINGFIELD. *(Thoughtfully.)* It is quite possible, you know, Inspector.

*(***BRENDA** *turns back to* **EMMELINE**.*)*

BRENDA. And you *do* hate her.

EMMELINE. Me? My own sister?

BRENDA. I've seen you looking at her often. You were in love with Bryan, he was half engaged to you and then Jenny came home from abroad and cut you out. Oh, she told me the whole story one day. You've never forgiven her. I think you've hated her ever since. I think that you came into her room that day and you saw her leaning over the balcony and it was too good a chance to be missed. You came up behind her and pushed her over!

EMMELINE. Inspector! Can't you stop this kind of thing?

INSPECTOR. I don't know that I want to, Miss Ross. I find it all very informative.

GINSBERG. I'm afraid I must insist on your leaving now. The patient must rest. We should be able to resume in twenty minutes. Nurse will take you downstairs.

NURSE. Yes, Doctor.

> *(She holds open the door.* **ROSS, EMMELINE, WINGFIELD** *and* **BRENDA** *move to exit.)*

INSPECTOR. Miss Ross, would you mind waiting a moment?

> *(They all pause briefly then* **BRENDA** *exits followed by* **ROSS,** *the* **NURSE** *and* **WINGFIELD.***)*

EMMELINE. Well, what is it?

> *(The* **INSPECTOR** *indicates a chair.* **EMMELINE** *sits.* **GINSBERG** *watches attentively.)*

INSPECTOR. There are one or two questions I should like to put to you. I didn't want to embarrass your brother.

EMMELINE. *(Sharply.)* Embarrass William? You don't know him. He has no self-respect at all. Never ashamed to admit that he doesn't know where to turn for the next penny!

INSPECTOR. *(Politely.)* That's very interesting but it was your brother-in-law that I thought might be embarrassed by the questions I am about to ask you.

EMMELINE. *(Surprised.)* Oh, Bryan. What do you want to know?

INSPECTOR. Miss Ross, you know the family very well. A person of your – intelligence would not be deceived as to what went on in it. You know the lives of your sister and your brother-in-law and what the relations were between them. It is reasonable that, up to now, you would say as little as you could. But now that you know what our suspicions are and the way they have been confirmed only a minute or two ago – well, that alters matters, doesn't it?

EMMELINE. Yes, I suppose it does. What do you want me to tell you?

INSPECTOR. This affair between Mr. Wingfield and Miss Jackson, was it serious?

EMMELINE. Not on his part. His affairs never are.

INSPECTOR. There actually *was* an affair?

EMMELINE. Of course. You heard her. She as good as admitted it.

INSPECTOR. You know it of your own knowledge?

EMMELINE. I could tell you various details to prove it but I do not propose to do so. You will have to accept my word for it.

INSPECTOR. It started when?

EMMELINE. Nearly a year ago.

INSPECTOR. And Mrs. Wingfield found out about it?

EMMELINE. Yes.

INSPECTOR. And what was her attitude?

EMMELINE. She taxed Bryan with it.

INSPECTOR. And he?

EMMELINE. He denied it, of course. Told her she was imagining things. You know what men are! Lie their way out of anything!

> *(The* **INSPECTOR** *and* **GINSBERG** *exchange a look.)*

She wanted him to send the girl away, but he wouldn't – said she was far too good a secretary to lose.

INSPECTOR. But Mrs. Wingfield was very unhappy about it?

EMMELINE. Very.

INSPECTOR. Unhappy enough to want to take her own life?

EMMELINE. Not if she'd been well and strong. But her illness got her down. And she got all kinds of fancies.

GINSBERG. *(Curiously.)* What kinds of fancies, Miss Ross?

EMMELINE. Just fancies.

INSPECTOR. Why was Mrs. Wingfield left alone that afternoon?

EMMELINE. She preferred it. One of us always offered to sit with her but she had her books and her radio. For some reason she preferred to be alone.

INSPECTOR. Whose idea was it to send the nurse off duty?

GINSBERG. In private nursing that's standard practice. She would have two hours off every afternoon.

INSPECTOR. Miss Jackson has told us that, "It was all over ages ago," referring to her affair with Mr. Wingfield. Do you say that was not so?

EMMELINE. I think they broke with each other for a while. Or possibly they were very careful. But at the time of the accident it was on again all right. Oh yes!

INSPECTOR. You seem very sure of that.

EMMELINE. I lived in the house, didn't I?

(She pauses.)

And I'll show you something.

(She takes a piece of paper out of her handbag and hands it to the **INSPECTOR**.*)*

I found it in the big Ming vase on the hall table. They used it as a post box it seems.

INSPECTOR. *(Reading.)* "Darling, we must be careful. I think she suspects. B."

(He looks at **GINSBERG**.*)*

EMMELINE. It's Bryan's writing all right. So, you see!

GINSBERG. Do you mind if I ask a question or two?

INSPECTOR. No Doctor, please do.

GINSBERG. I'm interested in those "fancies" you mentioned, Miss Ross. You had some particular fancy in mind, I think.

EMMELINE. Just a sick woman's imaginings. She was ill, you see and she felt she wasn't making the progress she should have done.

GINSBERG. And she thought there was a reason for that?

EMMELINE. She was – just upset.

(The **INSPECTOR** *leans forward, stressing his words.)*

INSPECTOR. She thought there was a reason for it.

EMMELINE. *(Uneasily.)* Well – yes.

GINSBERG. *(Quietly.)* She thought those two were poisoning her? That's it, isn't it?

(There is a pause.)

EMMELINE. *(Reluctantly.)* Yes.

GINSBERG. She said so to you?

EMMELINE. Yes.

GINSBERG. And what did you say?

EMMELINE. I told her it was all nonsense of course.

GINSBERG. Did you take any steps yourself?

EMMELINE. I don't know what you mean.

GINSBERG. Did you discuss it with the doctor attending her? Take any samples of food?

EMMELINE. *(Shocked.)* Of course not. It was just a sick woman's fancy.

GINSBERG. Well it happens, you know. Far more often than is known. The symptoms of arsenic poisoning, it's almost always arsenic, are practically indistinguishable from gastric disorders.

EMMELINE. Bryan couldn't – he just couldn't.

GINSBERG. It might have been the girl.

EMMELINE. Yes. Yes, I suppose so. *(Sighing.)* Well, we shall never know now.

GINSBERG. You're quite wrong there, Miss Ross. There are ways of telling. Traces of arsenic can be found in the hair, you know and in the finger nails.

EMMELINE. *(Rising.)* I can't believe it! I can't believe it of Bryan!

(She turns to the **INSPECTOR** *agitatedly.)*

Do you want me any longer, Inspector?

INSPECTOR. No, Miss Ross.

> (**EMMELINE** *holds out her hand for the paper she gave to the* **INSPECTOR**.)

INSPECTOR. I'll keep this. It's evidence.

EMMELINE. Yes, of course.

> (**EMMELINE** *exits.*)

GINSBERG. Well, we got something.

INSPECTOR. Yes.

> (*He sits in the elbow chair and looks at the piece of paper.*)

From the Ming vase in the hall. Interesting.

GINSBERG. It's his writing?

INSPECTOR. Oh yes, it's Bryan Wingfield's writing all right. You know, he was quite a one for the ladies. Bowled them over like ninepins. Unfortunately they always took him seriously.

GINSBERG. Doesn't strike me as the Casanova type. Writes all those historical novels. Very erudite.

INSPECTOR. There's quite a lot of dirt in history.

GINSBERG. So it wasn't all over!

INSPECTOR. Get four people all het up and accusing each other, get an embittered and malicious woman on her own and invite her to spill the beans. It gives one some material to work on, doesn't it?

GINSBERG. In addition to what you had already. What did you have?

INSPECTOR. (*Smiling.*) Just some good solid facts. I went into the financial angle. Bryan Wingfield's a poor man, his wife's a rich woman. Her life's insured in favour of him, not for a very large sum, but it would enable him to marry again if he wanted to. Her money came to her in trust. If she dies childless, it's divided between her brother and sister. The brother's a wastrel, always trying to get money out of his rich sister. According to Bryan, she told her brother she wasn't going to pay for him anymore. (*Thoughtfully.*) But I dare say she would have done – in the end.

GINSBERG. So which is it? B for Bryan? B for Brenda? B for Brother Bill? Or Emmeline without a B?

INSPECTOR. Emmeline without the – Emmeline? Wait a minute – something I heard this afternoon while they were all here.

(He pauses.)

No, it's gone.

GINSBERG. Could it be B for burglar?

INSPECTOR. No, that's definitely out. We've got conclusive evidence on that point. The road was up in front of the house and there was a constable on duty there. Both the side and the front gate were directly under his eye. Nobody entered or left the house, that afternoon.

GINSBERG. You know, you asked me to cooperate but you were very careful not to put all your cards on the table. Come on! What do you think?

INSPECTOR. It's not a question of thinking. I know.

GINSBERG. What?

INSPECTOR. I may be wrong, but I don't think so. You think it over.

(**GINSBERG** enumerates on his fingers.)

You've got seven minutes.

GINSBERG. Huh? Oh, yes.

(He rises and moves to the **PATIENT**. The **INSPECTOR** follows.)

Mrs. Wingfield. Thank you for your help, Mrs. Wingfield. We come now to the crucial moment in the experiment.

INSPECTOR. Mrs. Wingfield, we are about to leave you here, apparently unguarded. None of the suspects know that you regained your powers of speech yesterday. They don't know that you did not in fact see who pushed you off that balcony. You realise what that means?

PATIENT. One of them will – will try to –

INSPECTOR. Someone will almost certainly enter this room.

GINSBERG. Are you sure you want to go through with this, Mrs. Wingfield?

PATIENT. Yes, yes. I must know – I must know who –

INSPECTOR. Don't be afraid. We shall be close at hand. If anyone approaches you or touches you –

PATIENT. I know what to do.

INSPECTOR. Thank you, Mrs. Wingfield, you're a wonderful woman. Just be brave for a few moments longer and we shall trap our killer. Trust me. Trust both of us, eh?

GINSBERG. Ready?

INSPECTOR. Right.

> (GINSBERG *crosses to the doors and holds one open.*)

GINSBERG. Why don't you come into my office? In view of this poisoning suggestion you might like to look over the files.

INSPECTOR. Yes, I'd like another look at those X-ray plates too, if I may.

> (*He switches off the lights and they exit. There is a pause. In the darkness a figure is seen entering holding a small syringe and making straight for the* PATIENT.)

PATIENT. Help! Help!

> (*The figure quickly slips behind the recess curtain. The* INSPECTOR *enters.*)

INSPECTOR. All right, Mrs. Wingfield, we're here!

> (GINSBERG *follows. He switches on the lights.*)

PATIENT. Help! Murder!

> (*She points to the curtain.*)

There!

> (*The* INSPECTOR *looks to* GINSBERG.)

INSPECTOR. Is she all right?

GINSBERG. She's all right. You've been very brave, Mrs. Wingfield.

INSPECTOR. Thank you, Mrs. Wingfield. The killer has played right into our hands. That note in the Ming vase was all I needed. Bryan Wingfield would hardly need to write secret notes to a secretary he sees every day. He wrote that note to someone else. And that constable on duty. He swears that nobody entered or left the house that afternoon.

(He moves slowly to the curtain.)

So it seems you didn't take your off-duty walk that day. You may come out from behind that curtain now, Nurse Bond.

*(**NURSE BOND** emerges. Black out.)*

End of Play

THE AGATHA CHRISTIE COLLECTION

Agatha Christie is regarded as the most successful female playwright of all time. Her illustrious dramatic career spans forty-two years, countless acclaimed original plays, several renowned novels adapted for stage, and numerous collections of thrilling one-act plays. Testament to Christie's longevity, these plays continue to engage great artists and enthral audiences today.

Since the première of her first play in 1930 the world of theatre has changed immeasurably, and so has the way plays are published and performed. Embarking upon a two-year project, Agatha Christie Limited sought to re-open Christie's distinguished body of dramatic work, looking to both original manuscripts and the most recent publications to create a "remastered" edition of each play. Each new text would contain only the words of Agatha Christie (or adaptors she personally worked with) and all extraneous materials that might come between the interpreter and the playwright would be removed, ultimately bringing the flavor and content of the texts closer to what the author would have delivered to the rehearsal room. Each new edition would then be specifically tailored to the needs and requirements of the professional twenty-first century artist.

The result is The Collection.

Whether in a classic revival or new approach, The Collection has been purposely assembled for the contemporary theatre professional. The choice and combination of plays offers something for all tastes and kinds of performance with the skill, imagination and genius of Agatha Christie's work now waiting to be explored anew in theatre.

For more information on The Collection, please visit
agathachristielimited.com/licensing/stage/browse-by-play

9 780573 021985